MARCEL TAMINATO

Dare to Question

A JOURNAL FOR UPRISING

Preface

Ailton Krenak

Illustrations

Carla Miyasaka

Rayssa Oliveira

Revision

Daniel Hunter

Translation

Débora Gastal

DARE TO QUESTION

A JOURNAL FOR UPRISING

ISBN: 978-65-00-20478-0 (paperback)

ISBN: 978-65-00-20479-7 (ebook)

Cover, book design and illustrations

Carla Miyasaka

Rayssa Oliveira

Revision

Daniel Hunter

Translation

Débora Gastal

"Curiosity as a restless questioning, as a movement
toward the revelation of something hidden,
as a question verbalized or not, as a search for
clarity, as a moment of attention, suggestion, and
vigilance, constitutes an integral part of the
phenomenon of being alive.

There could be no creativity without curiosity
that moves us and sets us patiently impatient
before a world that we did not make,
to add to it something of our own making".

Paulo Freire,

Pedagogy of Freedom: Fundamental knowledges
for the educational practice, 1996.

Breaths of Life: The Summoning of the Seed

Ailton Krenak

Awakening the production of life from within us is wonderful. It is not an obligation, it is not an embarrassment. It is a radical freedom we own, to be able to choose starting life whenever we want.

This unrestrained capacity to produce life is the very experience that we share with other beings in this wonderful and indescribable living organism we call Gaia. But we get distracted, we get ill. And we forget about the whirlwind of life that is so alive that it escapes from our sight.

Instead of searching for life somewhere else, we can awaken from within us the vitality we are given when we arrive as a seed here on Earth. That vitaly that is a wonderful and irremovable unity that explodes in life, creates worlds and recharges all the Springs.

From within ourselves, we can awaken life, health, and impact those around us. And with that acupressure which starts somewhere inside myself like a creative wave, it spreads all around. It heals the sky's bosom, it heals the place where we are.

It is wonderful because everything exists from that tiny point that we can activate within ourselves. There is no whole without the place. And the place is an infinity of points that creates what is the whole.

So we need to work on ourselves, where each one of us is. We need to take consciousness. Acupressure, do the movement in that place where there's pain. Acupressure is a healing technique of care. After freeing that point, move on to another one. This movement dissolves in different places of this vast organism that is Earth, those energies that are blocked and are creating fear, anguish and becoming a disease.

The urgency that surrounds us, this feeling of immobility in the face of such an enormous crisis, can take away our vital energy, our life zing and our ability to produce affection. This is not out there, outside.

The source of the creative life energy depends on us meeting the place where we are and reconciling ourselves with this wonderful life experience which we are called upon to perform.

When we find deserts in front of us, we must not run, but cross them. Life is insurgency, it is not accommodation. We will be seeds in the world and life triggers wherever we are - anywhere, in that place that is ours.

March 9, 2020

Excerpted from a class given at "o lugar", with permission.

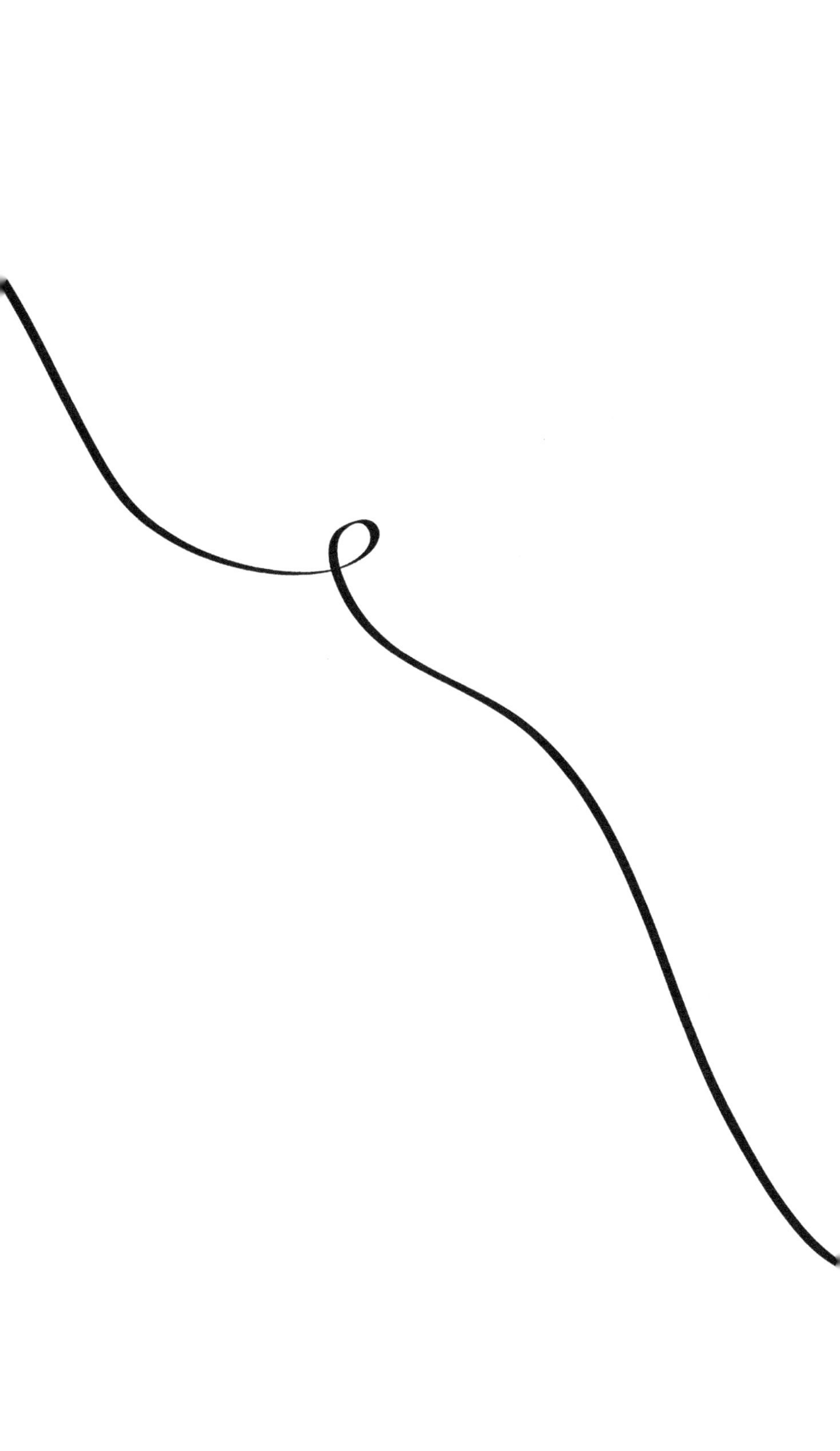

Grounding our existence

If what exists prevents us from being free, we have to question what gets in our way. This questioning approach is the basis of any effective transformative action: the action of refusing to surrender to unquestionable truths and of actively not conforming, to change a world that is turned upside down.

Through a continuously questioning and reflective nature of activism we better understand what is at stake and restlessly move outside our comfort zones to promote transformations. This intentional unlearning helps us to rescue our human potential to build other realities. After all, what do we want to keep? What do we want to change?

The call to guarantee our right to a future has never been more important. We have already reached the planetary limits that condition and support our existence. We need everyone, together and right now, to face an urgent task: to safeguard our basic right to revolt - to create for ourselves a new world.

Other possible futures need to be imagined, beyond the dystopian horizons so widespread in such arid times. It needs to start with our right to think free, to think that we can be more - as Paulo Freire said, when referring to freedom as an imperative to our existence. Cultivating our precious ability to question is a way to reactivate our curiosity and our restless practice of challenging the status quo.

Given the depth and scale of the crisis we are experiencing, we cannot postpone what is required of us: facing the climate emergency, the historic task of our time. We need to break the inertia of indifference and to collectively overcome the feeling of helplessness in the face of the magnitude of this problem.

Over the years, our childish resourcefulness to explore the world through questions has been restricted and labeled as an inconvenience, a defect, a disease and even a crime. By killing our ability to question, assumptions become certainties at the speed of a click. It feels like being surrendered to the inconvenience of not being able to be truly free, serves as an invitation to the dangerous proliferation of followers of unique systems of truth.

Questioning is an
antidote against attitudes of
indifference, empty speeches,
subjugation values, fatalistic lullabies,
authoritarian behaviors, superficial
arguments and dogmatic
generalizations.

Questioning rescues us, offers us an embryo of freedom so that we are not paralyzed by a culture of political impotence and by the fatalistic ideology of "the end of history". Anything can be questioned.

The following questions were generated by activists in learning processes around the world in recent years. It may be liberating to share these, humbly knowing that they may deepen our impulses for transformative interventions in the world.

A most inconvenient question posed to us at this point is about our ability to respond to a threat to our own existence. As the so deeply missed Uruguayan poet Eduardo Galeano wrote, "how about we begin to exercise the never-proclaimed right to dream? How about we rave for a moment?".

It is up to us to be bold.

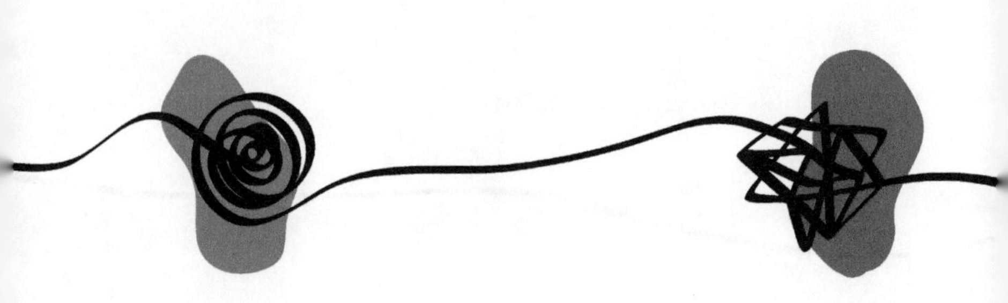

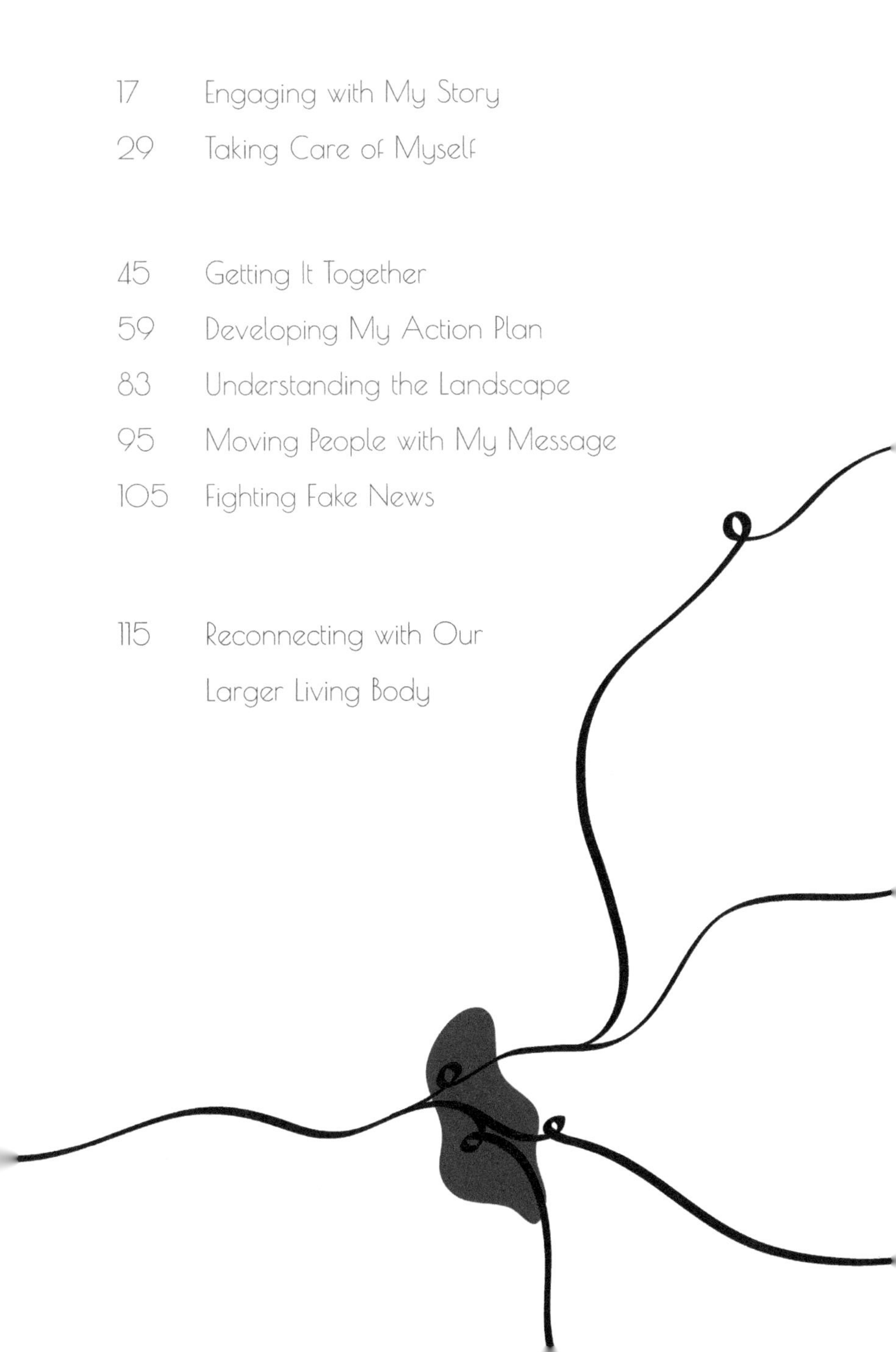

"The question that moves me is how each person invents a life. How do each of us create meaning for our days, almost naked and with so little. How do each of us wrest ourselves out of the silence, to become narrative. How do each of us inhabit ourselves".

Eliane Brum

My Mishappenings: The Story of My Life with the Words, 2014.

WAKING UP

the archeology of my fight

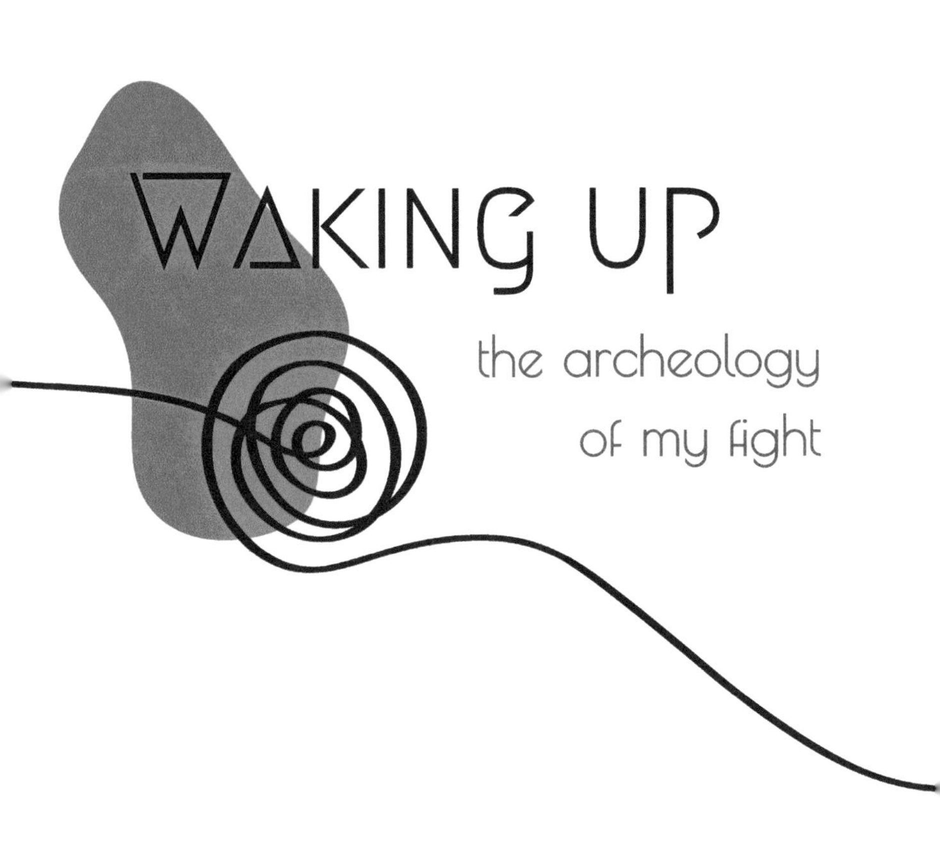

Engaging with My Story

WHEN DID YOUR STORY START?

Do you identify with any

POLITICAL TRADITION?

How does it influence your way

of thinking and acting?

How do you characterize your effort

to promote change?

Is it a **RESISTANCE** against setbacks,

or is it focused on **SOLUTIONS?**

Does it focus on **SPECIFIC** issues,

or does it address **STRUCTURAL** problems?

Is it based on **PAIN**

or on **LOVE?**

Is it connected to the **PAST**,

or oriented towards the **FUTURE?**

Is it based on what

YOU LIKE TO DO.

or on what

NEEDS TO BE DONE?

How do **YOUR WORDS**

relate to your actions?

Do **YOUR DREAMS**

speak to your actions?

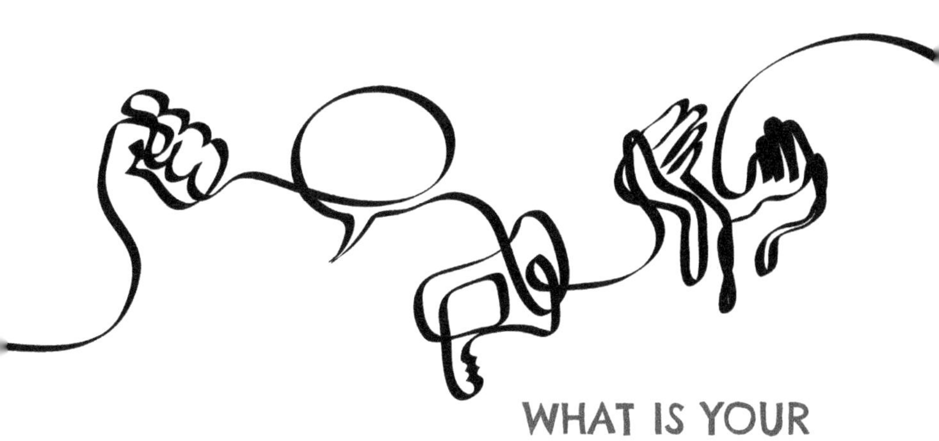

WHAT IS YOUR ACTIVIST PROFILE?

confrontation, negotiation,

mobilization, support.

How does creativity feed into

YOUR POTENTIAL?

What increases your

feeling of helplessness?

Is your activism different from

other kinds of search for transformation?

What do you mean by transformation?

When does the transformation take place?

How does the transformation happen?

What do you want to transform?

How can we see if there was a transformation?

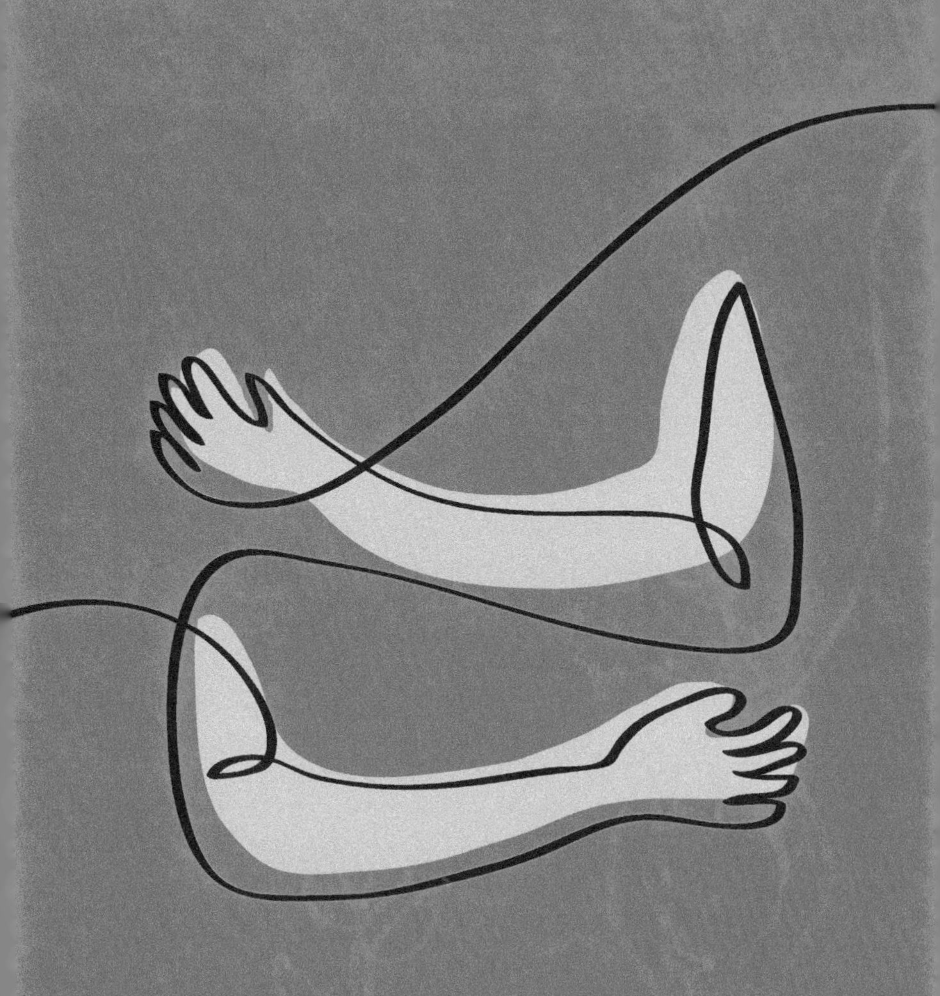

Taking Care of Myself

What keeps

your flame burning?

How to recover

the lost enthusiasm

after a long journey?

How do you

FEED YOUR ENERGY?

What do you do when

you feel powerless?

HOW ARE YOU TAKING CARE OF YOUR physical, mental and spiritual HEALTH?

What reasons may keep you from prioritizing your health care?

When do you know you are not well and need to take a break?

Why prepare psychologically?

Why exercise physically?

How do you deal with frustration,

boredom, tiredness, stress?

How have you been dealing

with your fear and anxiety?

ARE THERE LIMITS

in the name of a cause?

ARE THERE ANY BOUNDARIES

between your personal life

and your political work?

What puts you in motion,

CRITICISM

or **PRAISE?**

What's more important:

the **PEOPLE**

you work with

or the **CAUSE**

you stand for?

What would you like to do but are still lacking the **COURAGE?**

What would you be willing to give up?

How does **POWER** influence you?

How does money influence you?

Who funds you and where does
the **MONEY** come from?

WHAT CAN ONLY YOU DO?

How much have you been dedicated?

If you stopped doing what you are doing, what would change?

Why leave the comfort zone?

When you leave the comfort zone,

what do you do to stay grounded?

IS IT POSSIBLE TO CHANGE THE WORLD WITHOUT CHANGING YOURSELF?

Have you

REFLECTED ON

your experiences?

Have you learned from

YOUR MISTAKES?

How to deal with

very difficult questions?

WHY DO YOU STOP ASKING QUESTIONS?

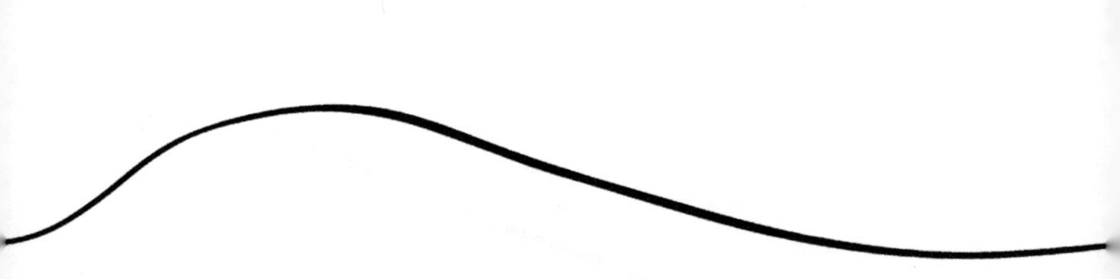

"To say no to the bad ideas and bad actors is simply not enough. The firmest of the nos come with a bold and progressive yes, a plan for the future that is credible and attractive enough for a large number of people to fight to see it happening. No may be what will initially take millions to the streets. But it is the yes that will keep us in the fight. The yes is the lighthouse in the storms to come, that will prevent us from getting lost".

Naomi Klein

No Is Not Enough: Resisting Trump's Shock Politics and Winning the World We Need, 2017.

ORGANIZING
the power of our
collective action

Getting It Together

Who is **YOUR COMMUNITY?**

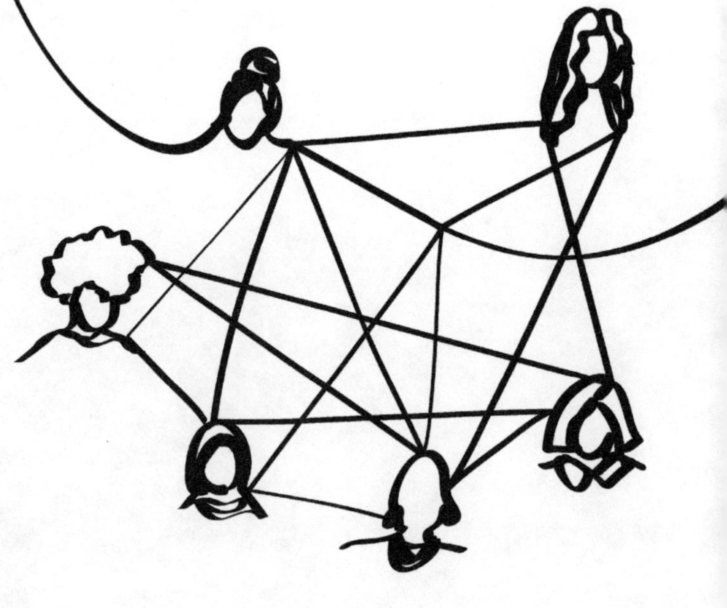

Who normally speaks for your community?

WHO DO YOU TRUST

to have the best interests of your community?

How do you know you trust them?

Do others in your community trust them?

How do people gain trust in your community?

HOW DOES YOUR COMMUNITY ORGANIZE ITSELF already?

Do you believe we should always organize **HORIZONTALLY?**

Do you believe we should always organize **VERTICALLY?**

Should we build and grow **FORMAL INSTITUTIONS?**

Should we follow more **EPHEMERAL ORGANIZATION DYNAMICS?**

Should we be guided by

the opportunities that

ARISE SPONTANEOUSLY?

Should we be guided by

PLANNED ACTIONS over time?

How do your preferences interfere

in the way you act in community?

Why should we talk about

COLLABORATION?

Why should we talk about

NON-COOPERATION?

Which do you prefer talking about?

How does your community

decide to change its situation?

How has it done it in the past?

What does a "movement"

look like to your community?

What actions show a movement of change

is happening in your community?

When does it

make sense to talk about

LEADERSHIP?

How does the

appropriation of causes by leaders

WEAKEN THE MOVEMENT?

How do leaders

STRENGTHEN THE MOVEMENT?

How do you know when you see

someone with leadership?

How do you know when you have it?

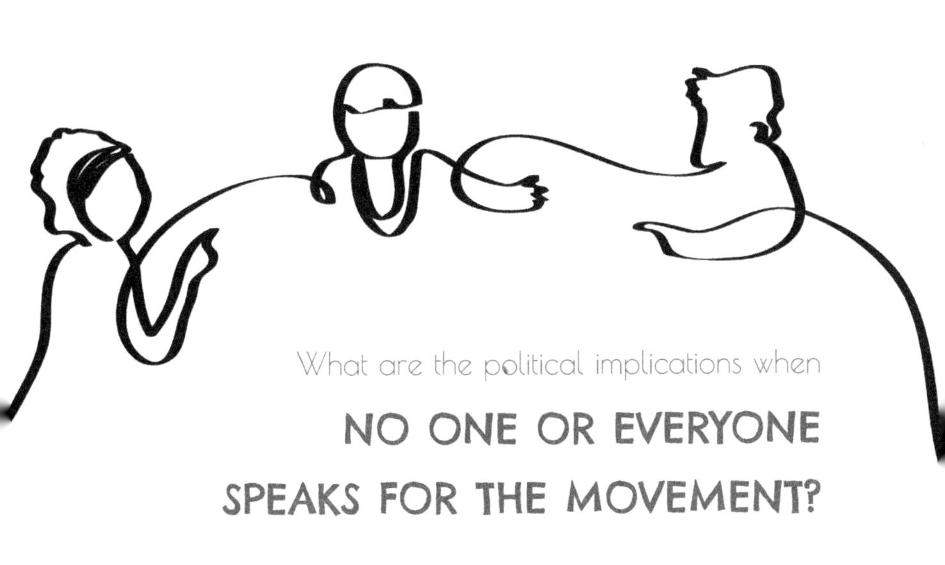

What are the political implications when

NO ONE OR EVERYONE SPEAKS FOR THE MOVEMENT?

Why is the

DIVISION OF ROLES

important?

What roles are essential?

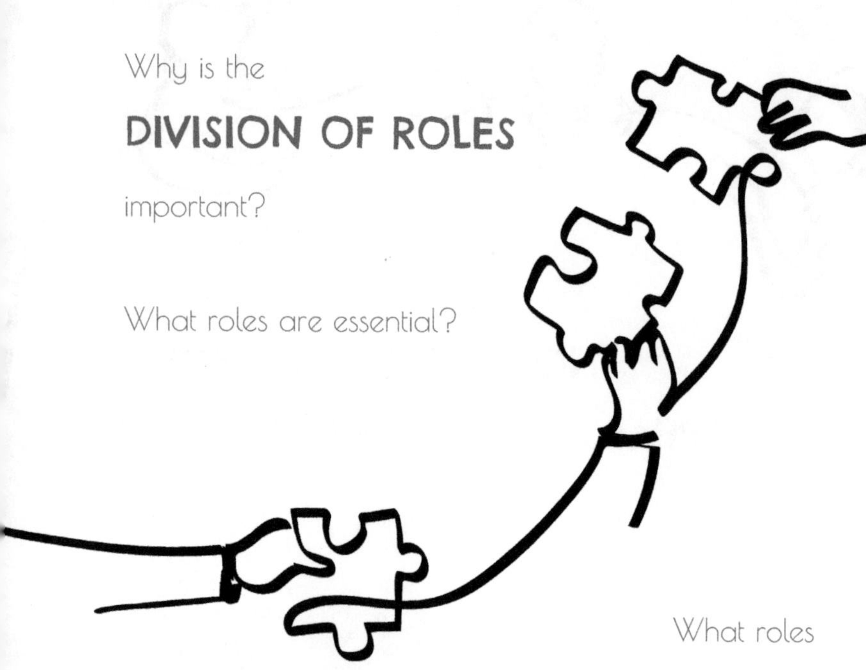

What roles

do you most like playing?

What role do you least like playing?

How does the way you were raised

limit the roles you play?

What strengthens the

SENSE OF BELONGING

to the collective?

How do you hinder a community culture?

How does a complaining culture

hinder collective action?

What happens when the

COLLECTIVE IDENTITY

is stronger than the

commitment to the cause?

What keeps your

COMMITMENT TO A CAUSE?

What maintains

PEOPLE'S SUPPORT?

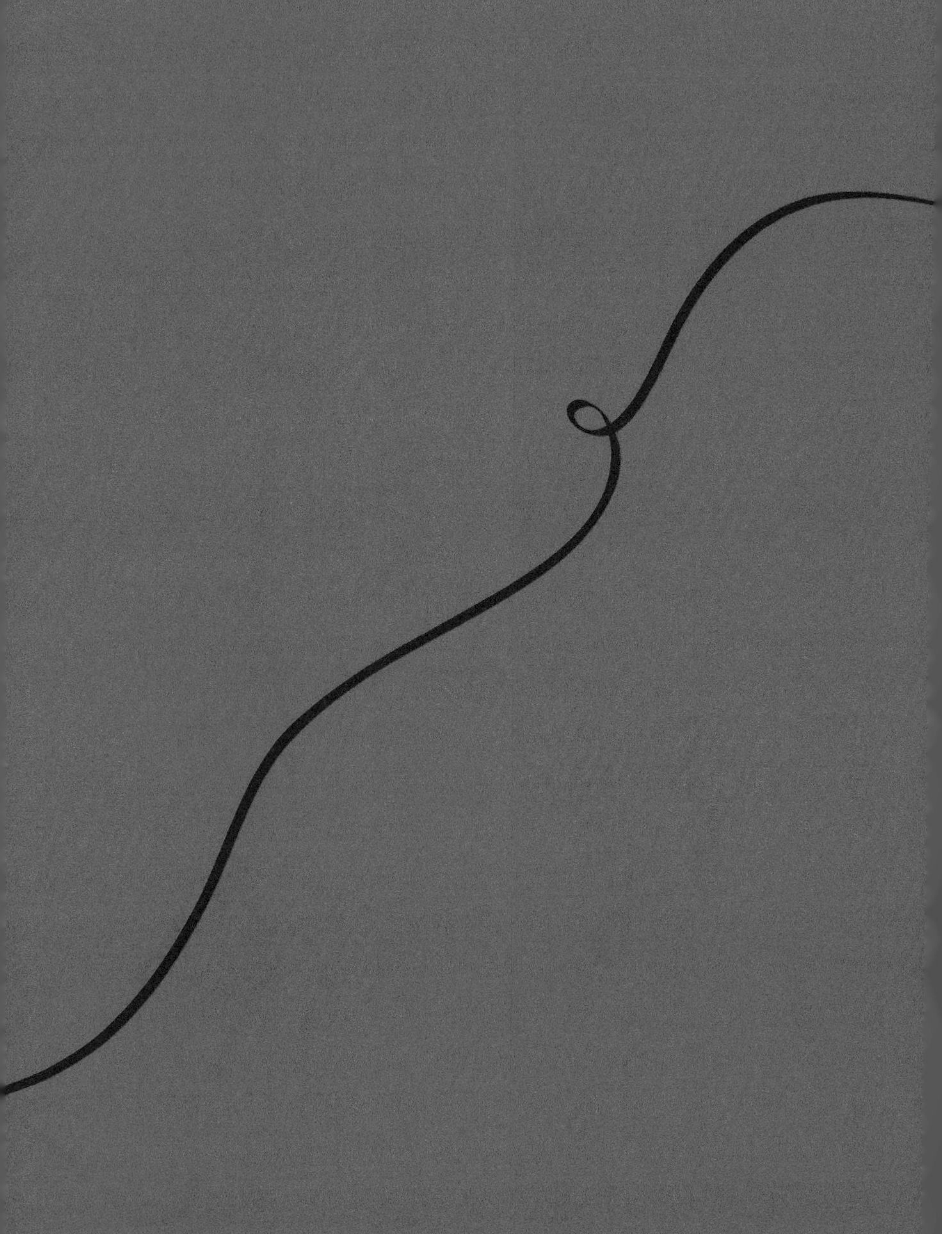

Developing My Action Plan

What suffering does your community

assume it has to put up with?

How does your community

decide it has had enough?

WHAT MOBILIZES PEOPLE FOR ACTION?

How do you get support

and involve more people?

How do you mobilize in a scenario

of uncertainty and rapid changes?

What are everyday

ACTS OF RESISTANCE

that go unnoticed?

Why do they go **UNNOTICED?**

Do they matter if they are unnoticed?

What makes an action matter?

How does acting collectively

change power dynamics?

What do you

WANT TO CHANGE?

WHAT IS IN DISPUTE?

How do you

IDENTIFY A PROBLEM

people are ready to change?

How do you identify the problem needs to be fixed

even when people are not ready to change?

Why does that problem persist?

What is its **CAUSE?**

What is its **CONSEQUENCE?**

How to prioritize what to do?

When is the best time to act?

How long should the action last?

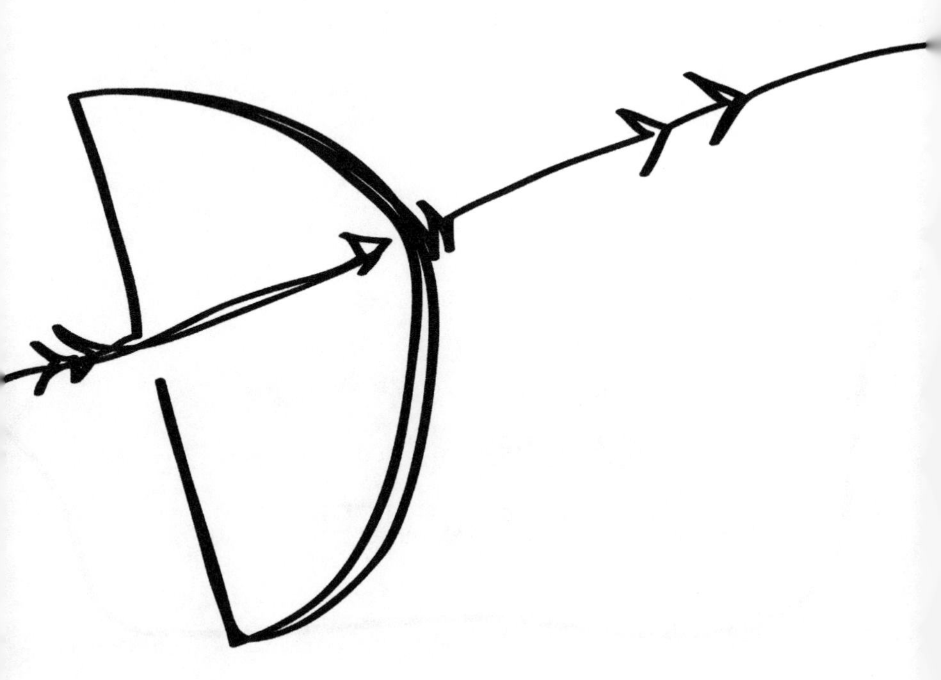

WHAT HAS TO CHANGE

for the problem to end?

WHO HAS TO CHANGE

for the problem to end?

Why is it essential to

OCCUPY STREETS AND OTHER PUBLIC SPACES

in person with other people?

When does public pressure play a crucial role?

How can outrage, joy, resentment, love, hope and despair constitute different processes of mobilization?

What mobilizes people more:

the **OUTRAGE AGAINST INJUSTICE**

or the **HOPE FOR JUSTICE?**

What is more important: who mobilizes, why people mobilize, or that people are mobilized?

On what occasions can reporting and exposure of serious cases lead to mobilization?

What are **ACTIONS** that have been

REALLY EFFECTIVE?

Is it according to the intended change?

Is it according to the time needed

to reach your goal?

Is it according to the available resources?

Which actions do you actually do?

Is it according to what you've done before?

Is it according to what will make you feel good?

Is it according to what is safest for your community?

DO THE ENDS JUSTIFY THE MEANS?

Why improvise if you can plan?

Why wait if you can act now?

WHY DO AN ACTION only once?

Why do an action multiple times?

Why do an action at the
same time in different places?

Why do an action in only one place?

WHY DO NOT TAKE ACTION?

Why take action quickly?

Why do you persist
with the same action?

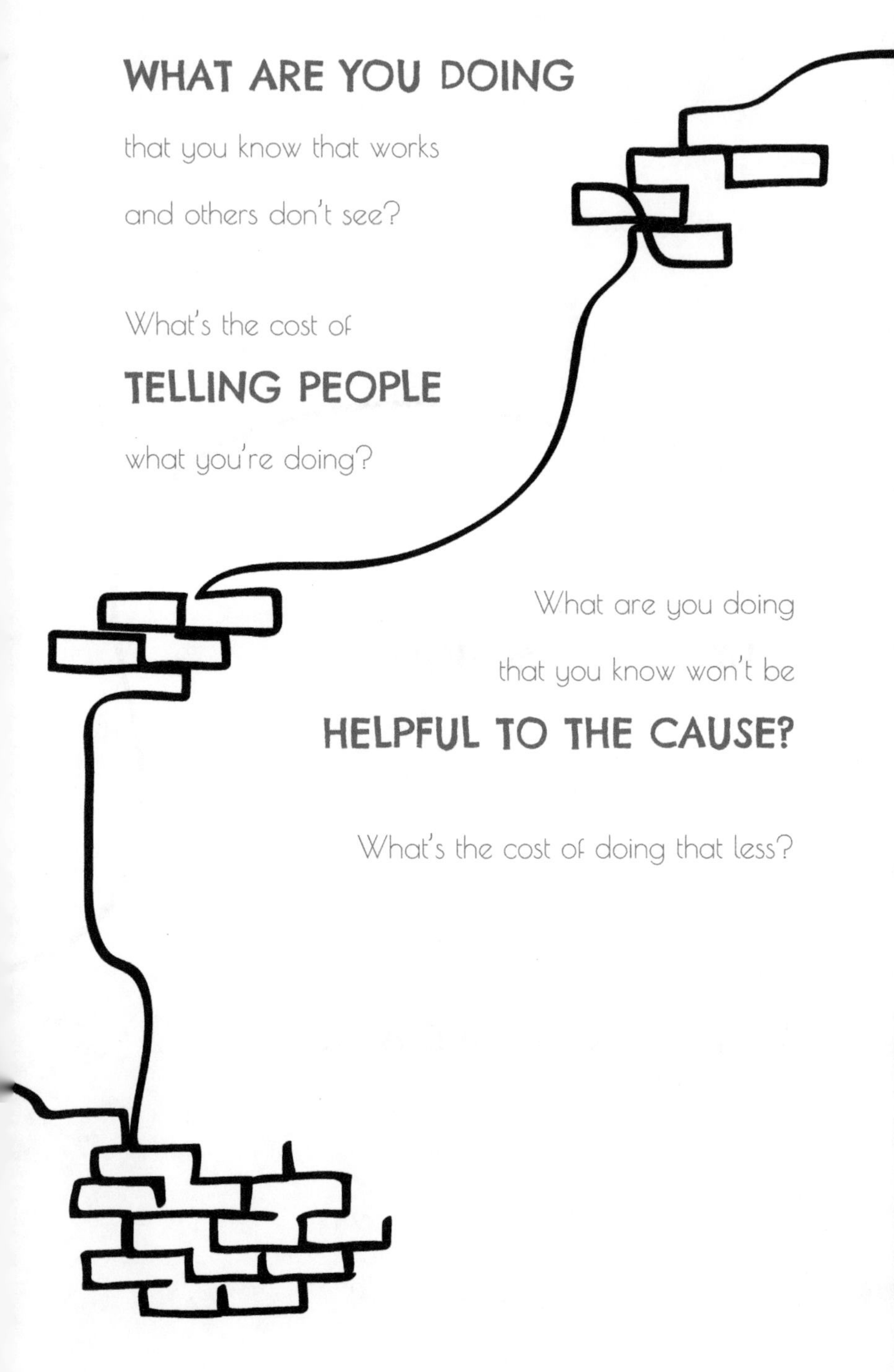

WHAT ARE YOU DOING

that you know that works

and others don't see?

What's the cost of

TELLING PEOPLE

what you're doing?

What are you doing

that you know won't be

HELPFUL TO THE CAUSE?

What's the cost of doing that less?

How to maintain **FOCUS** and **SPIRIT?**

What to do in the face of negative reactions?

And the positive?

When do you

USE HUMOR

effectively?

When do you

RAISE AWARENESS

effectively?

When do you

CAUSE EMBARRASSMENT

effectively?

When do you

PUT PRESSURE

effectively?

What

LEGAL RISKS

do you want to take?

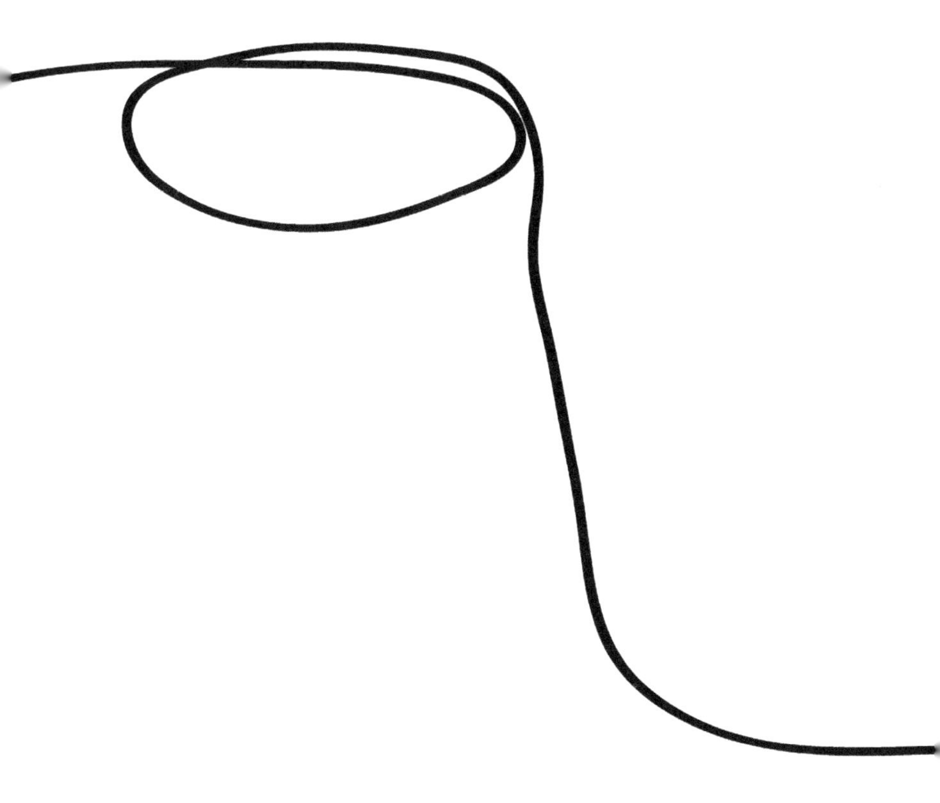

Why is the **END** of an action

as important as its **BEGINNING?**

How do you know if an action is helping

ACHIEVE YOUR GOAL?

How do you actually feel after an

EFFECTIVE ACTION?

How can we avoid being

held hostage to specific

ACHIEVEMENTS?

How do you know

PROGRESS

is being made?

Why should we always

EVALUATE our practice?

How does **SELF-CRITICISM** serve you?

When does self-criticism get in your way?

When does **PRAISE** foster motivation?

When does it become a naive celebration?

Which do you

tend towards?

How can the power

of spontaneous actions

help in the process for

SYSTEMIC CHANGE?

What to do when

the planned action fails?

Why should we

CELEBRATE THE ACHIEVEMENTS

obtained?

Who celebrates

achievements in your life

with you?

Understanding the Landscape

Do you look at things

ANALYTICALLY or

WITH YOUR HEART?

What's the difference?

Why **ANALYZE** the situation?

When have

EXTERNAL FACTORS

forced you to change your plan?

Did you see them coming?

Do you normally see them coming?

How can you raise your vision

to see more of them?

What external factors can influence your plan?

WHAT ASPECTS TO CONSIDER?

political, economic, social, technological,

environmental and legal.

What are the

OPPORTUNITIES?

What are the

THREATS?

What are your

STRENGTHS?

What are your

WEAKNESSES?

Who benefits from my actions?

Who can help you?

Who can block your way?

Who will sabotage you?

Who will resist you?

Who are your **ALLIES?**

Who are your **OPPONENTS?**

How do you know who is who?

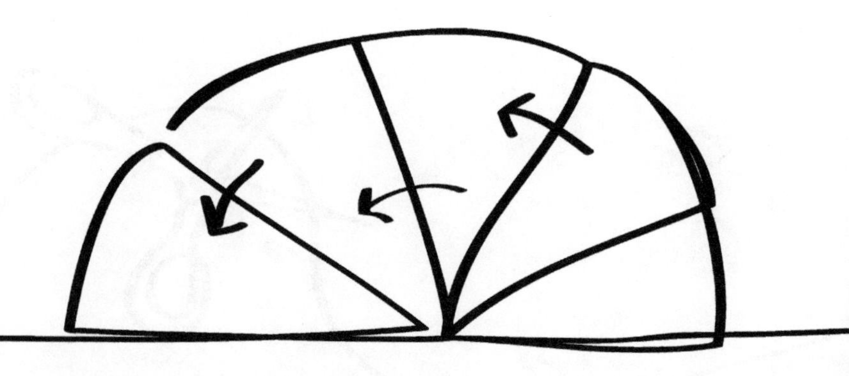

WHO AND WHERE IS YOUR REAL OPPONENT?

Who do your allies relate to?

And your opponents?

What mobilizes your allies?

And your opponents?

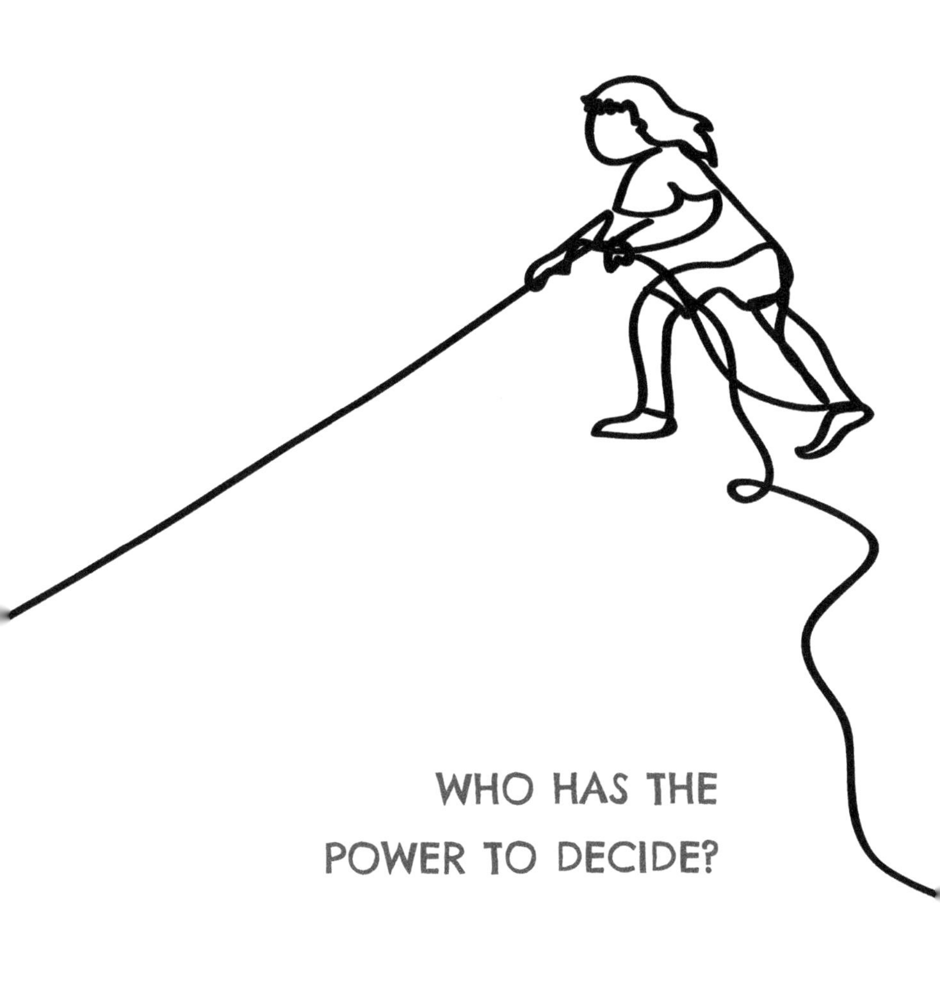

WHO HAS THE POWER TO DECIDE?

Who supports the decision-maker?

Who has control over resources and information?

Who has influence over whom?

Who depends on whom?

Which parts of the landscape are critical for **YOUR SUCCESS?**

Of these, which are you least interested in?

How could you get more interested in it?

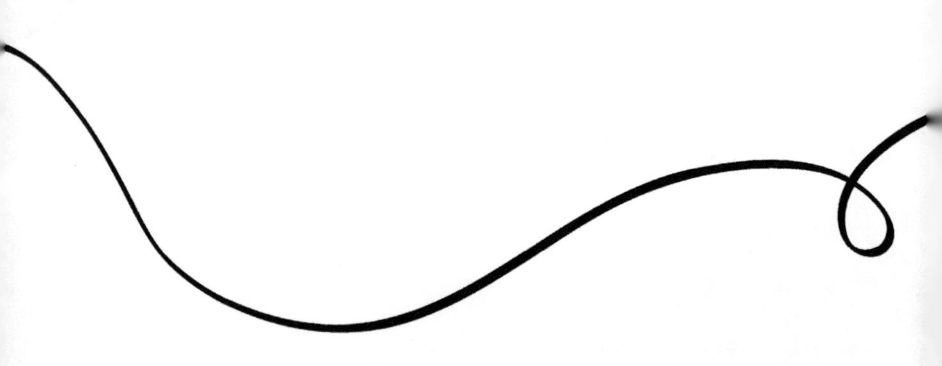

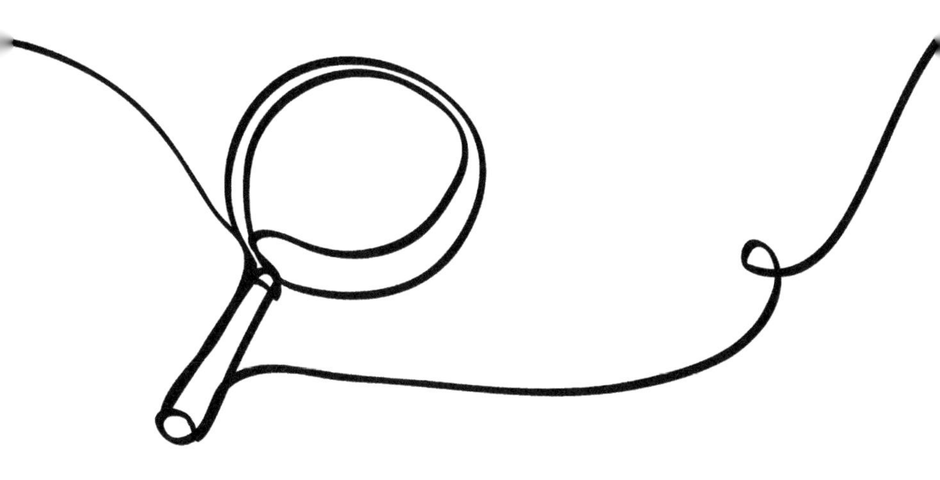

Moving People with My Message

What **VALUES** are most precious to **YOUR MESSAGE?**

What values precious to you do you have that others in your circle don't share?

What values overlap with people you haven't won over?

What message do you want to communicate?

What is your target audience?

How to adapt your message

to your **TARGET AUDIENCE?**

What values do you want

to promote and activate?

What do you need to do to win

PUBLIC SUPPORT?

When to win the support of public opinion?

How does

PUBLIC OPINION

see what you do?

How to increase pressure with

the support of public opinion?

How to choose media channels to

SPREAD YOUR MESSAGE?

When to leaflet on the streets

and when to post on the internet?

How to make the best use of social media?

How to engage more people on social media?

When to keep an open channel with allied press?

How is community media an important channel?

How to amplify your message
through the **MEDIA?**

Why create your own media?

What changes when anyone
can become their own media outlet?

How does the media view activism?

Why to act in partnership with the media?
Why not?

When is it important to leak information?

How to monitor what goes on in the

PRESS AND SOCIAL MEDIA?

How do algorithms shape and manipulate

your activism?

When can being in the media or

appearing on "trending topics" be alienating?

How effective is the use of memes?

How to protect yourself from media hijacking the **LOGIC OF THE SPECTACLE?**

What to do when **ACTIVISM** becomes an **OBJECT OF CONSUMPTION?**

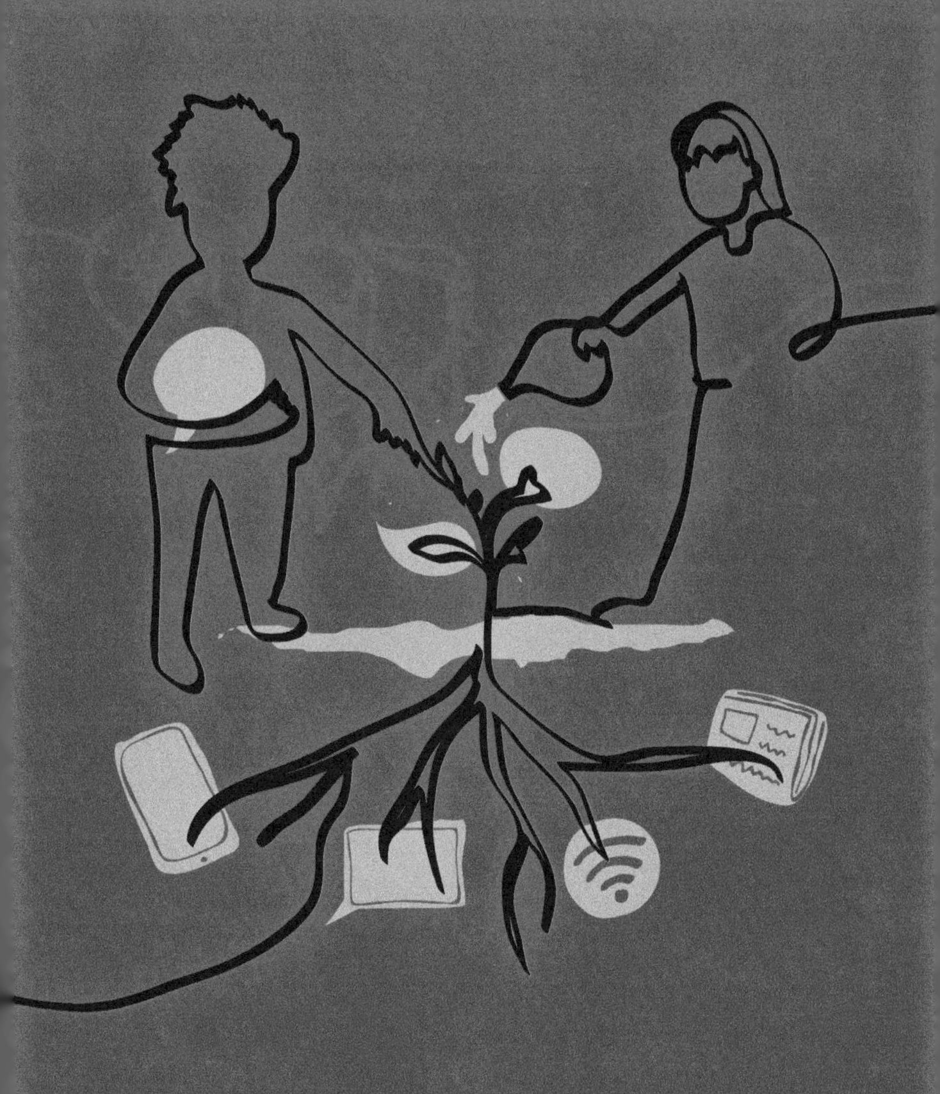

Fighting Fake News

How to deal with the sophistication

of the **FAKE NEWS** industry?

How does the "likes industry" promote

DISINFORMATION?

How to deal with vociferous harmful

campaign conspiracies?

How is the **MANIPULATION**

of numbers used against your cause?

How to deal with the risks of manipulation?

How do we filter what really matters,

considering the excess of information available?

How to know if information is credible?

Why act based on credible

and high-quality information?

How to maintain a network of

credible information sources?

How to escape from the

SUPERFICIAL DEBATE?

How to work with technical information

without alienating and demobilizing people?

For what purpose was that specific information produced and disseminated?

Why is that specific **INFORMATION** not **PUBLIC?**

Why isn't that specific **DATA OPEN?**

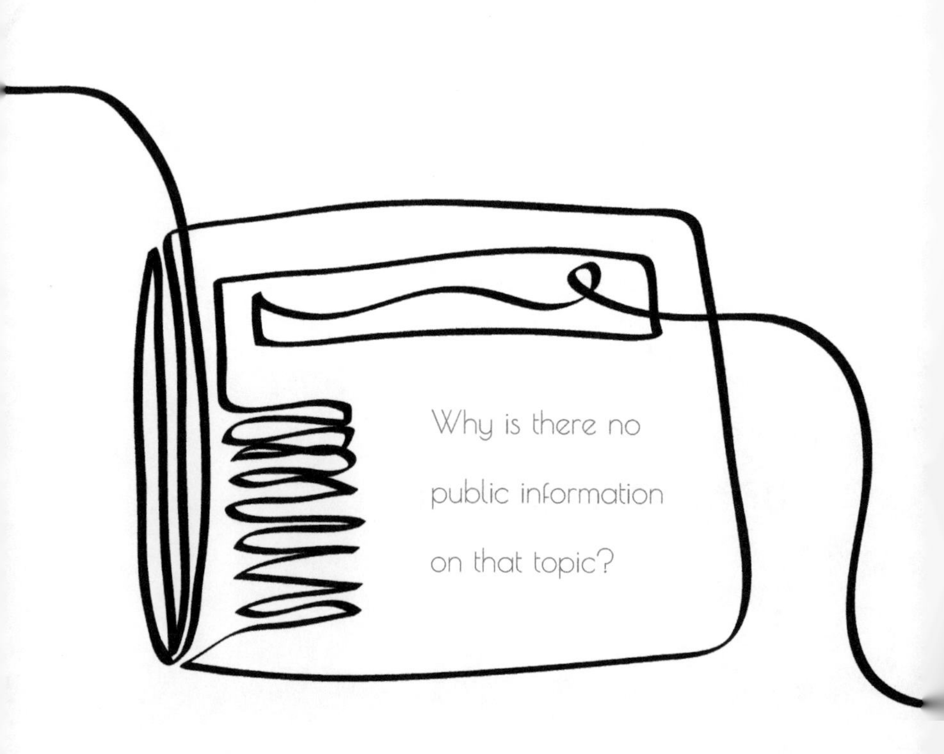

Why is there no public information on that topic?

How can **TRANSPARENCY** over your own information serve as a defense strategy?

How to benefit from the large amount of

DATA AVAILABLE?

How to protect ourselves from digital vulnerabilities?

How do you protect your computer
from malicious programs and hackers?

How to destroy sensitive information?

How to recover data?

HOW TO KEEP YOUR DATA SAFE?

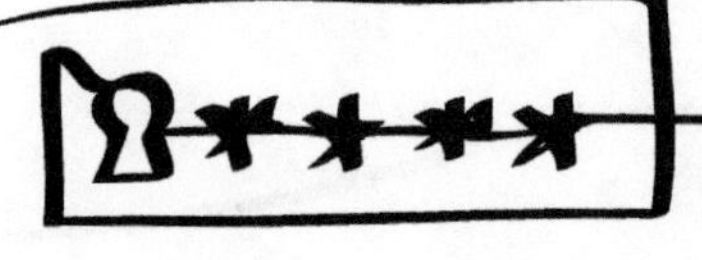

How to deal with the violation

of your digital privacy?

How do you protect

your sensitive files and important data?

How to use phones and smartphones safely?

How to browse safely on the internet?

How to create and keep passwords secure?

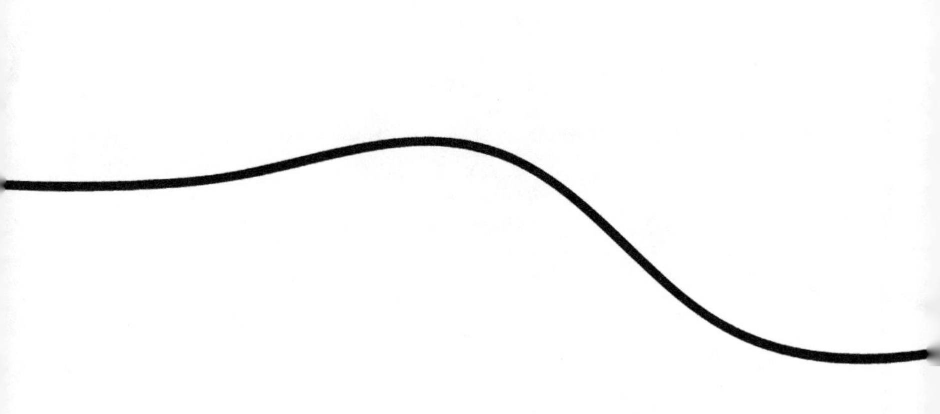

"When you feel like the sky is getting too low,
you just need to pull it up so you can breathe".

Ailton Krenak

Ideas to Postpone the End of the World, 2019.

Liberating

the world of civilizational crisis

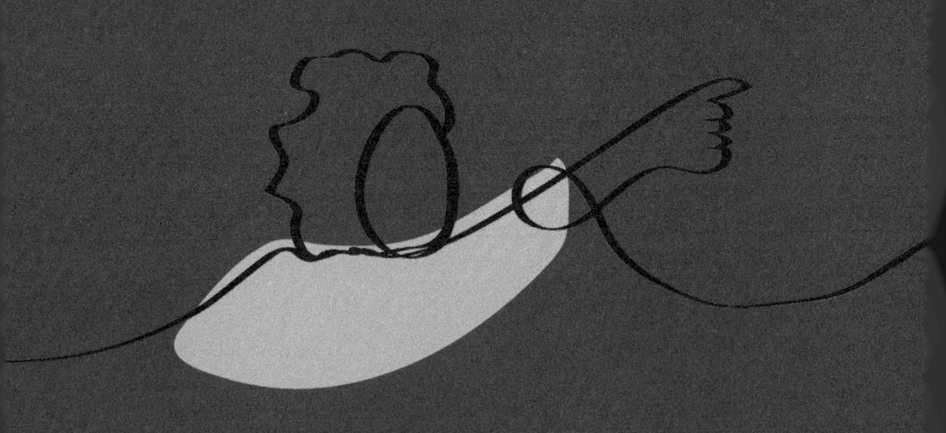

Reconnecting with Our Larger Living Body

WHY AREN'T WE FIGHTING TOGETHER?

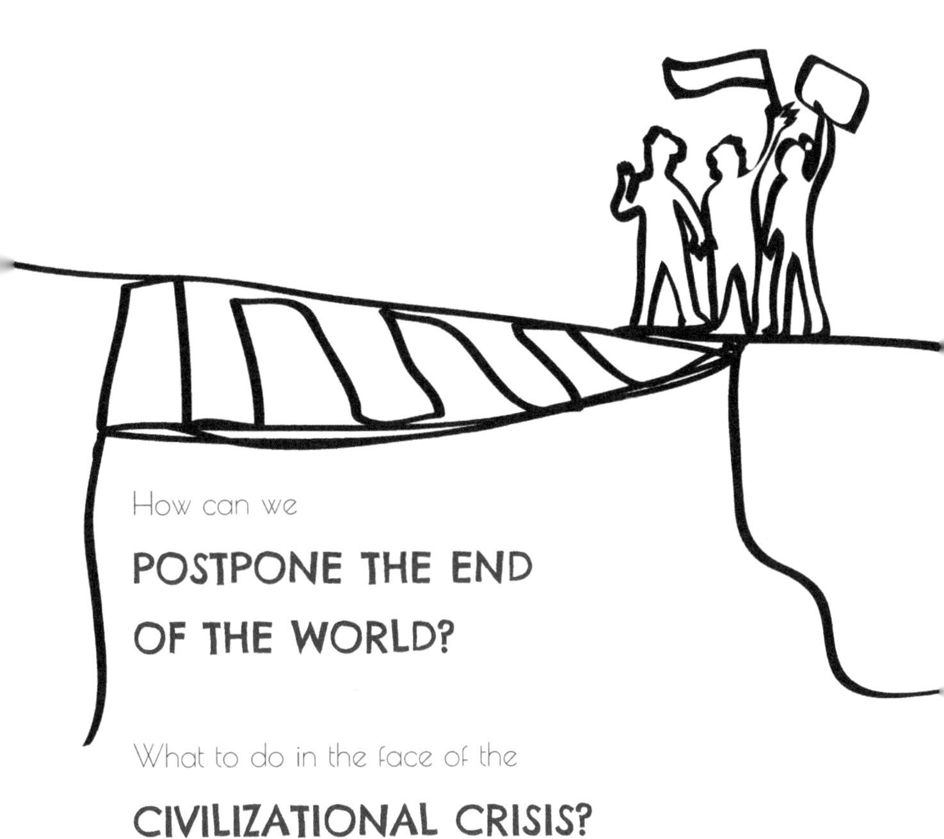

How can we

POSTPONE THE END OF THE WORLD?

What to do in the face of the

CIVILIZATIONAL CRISIS?

How

DID WE GET HERE?

What

HAVE WE DONE TO CHANGE?

Have we

LOST?

Are we

WINNING?

Why do we continue to

Why do we **NEGLECT ANCESTRAL KNOWLEDGE?**

Why do we **IGNORE** the alerts from **SCIENCE?**

Why is there so much **INEQUALITY?**

Why is there so much **VIOLENCE?**

Why is there so much **INJUSTICE?**

How to overcome ignorance?

How to face **AUTHORITARIANISM?**

How to fight **RACISM? SEXISM?**
ABLEISM? HOMOPHOBIA?

How to protest against abstract economic ideas

without looking completely outdated?

What should we do in the face of

the toxic polarization?

How to face the far right rise

around the world?

WHAT CAN WE LEARN

from the stories of struggle of the past?

What do we need to

DO DIFFERENTLY

from other times in history?

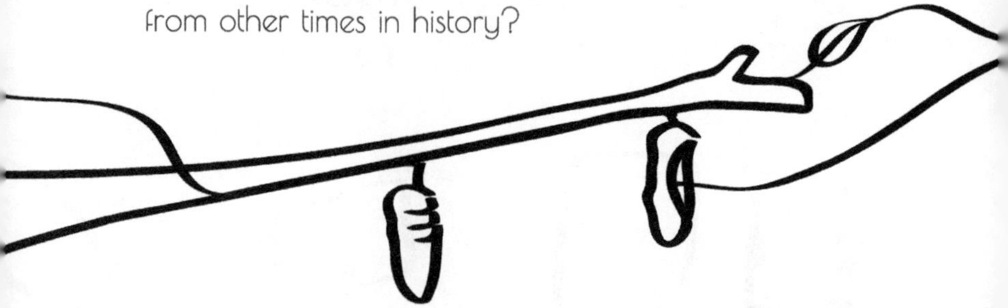

Where are the

NEW SPACES
OF RESISTANCE?

Where are the

NEW FORMS
OF EXISTENCE?

What kind of change

do we want to see in the world?

WHERE TO START FROM?

ARE THERE CAUSES THAT ARE MORE IMPORTANT THAN OTHERS?

How to face injustices

inside the social movements themselves?

Where is solidarity?

What have we done with **OUR FREEDOM?**

Do we really need heroes?

WHERE'S the power?

How to reaffirm **OUR POWER?**

Have we lost courage?

HOW MUCH TIME DO WE HAVE LEFT?

What do your ancestors tell you?

Are there reasons to keep **HOPE** alive?

Where are the **NEW UTOPIAS?**

What does **HISTORY** teach us?

Why is the **FUTURE** calling us?

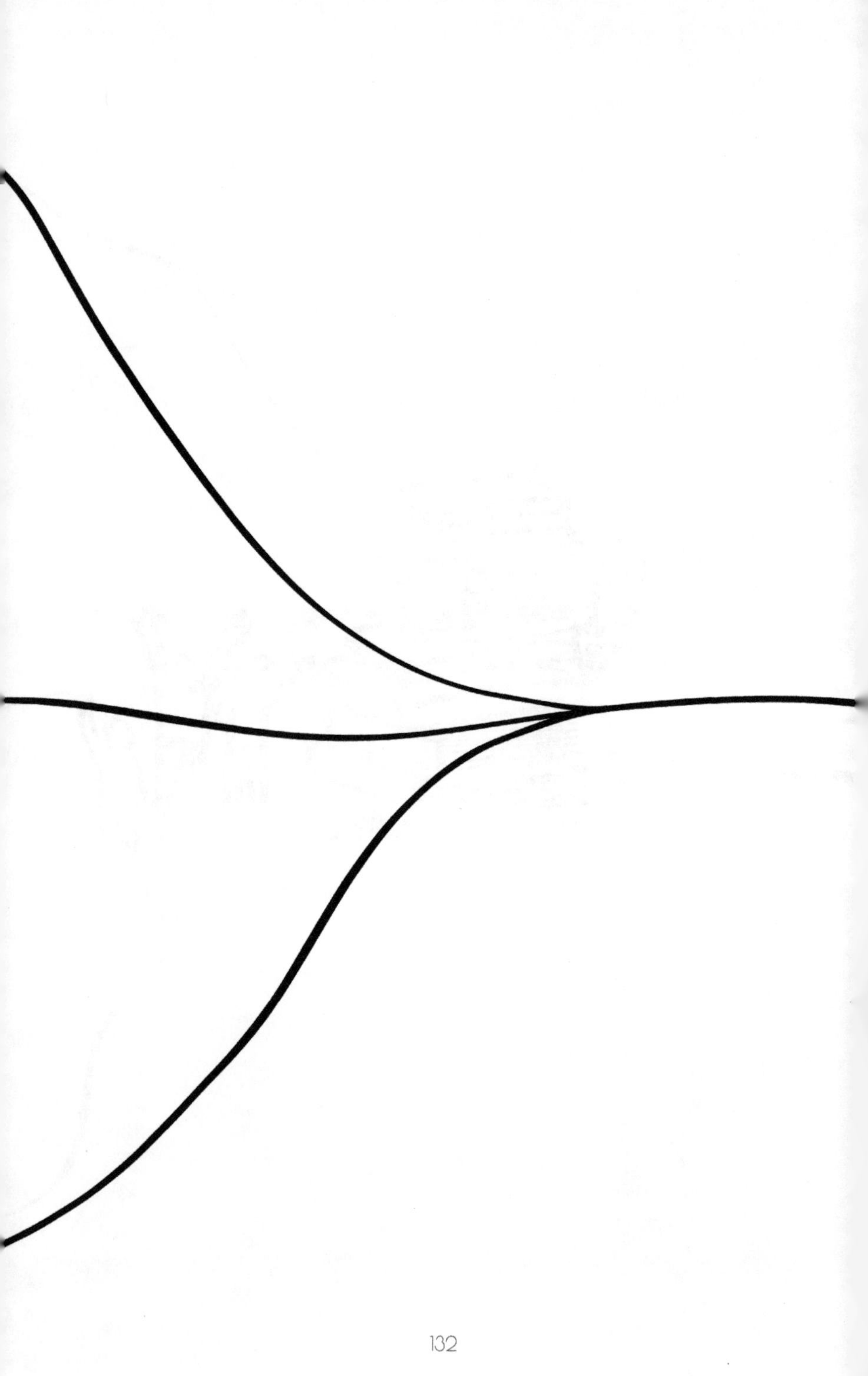

What is **MORE IMPORTANT NOW?**

MARCEL TAMINATO is Global Training Coordinator at 350.org. He contributed to the creation and growth of diverse organisations and movements around the world, with his experience in facilitation, organizing and strategy. He is the co-founder of School of Activism, in Brazil, and co-editor of the book Beautiful Rising: Creative Resistance from the Global South.

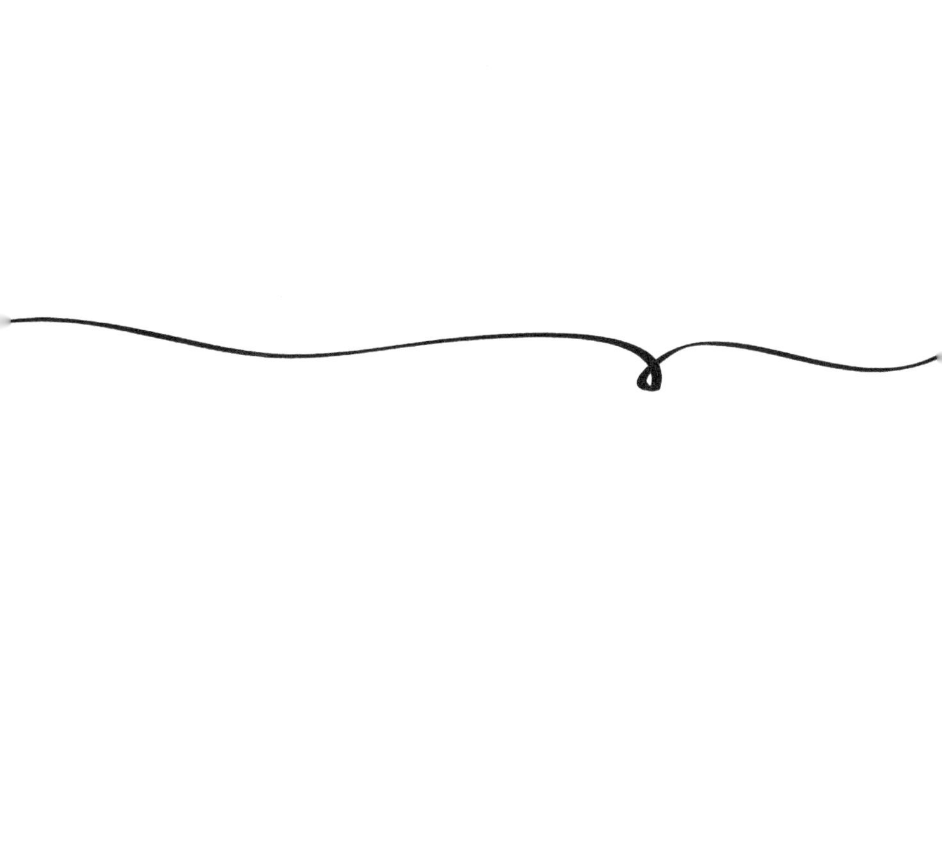